YOUR AUTOBIOGRAPHY

Poems

MERCER
UNIVERSITY

MERCER UNIVERSITY PRESS

Endowed by

TOM WATSON BROWN
and
THE WATSON-BROWN FOUNDATION, INC.

Your Autobiography

Poems

KELLY CHERRY

MERCER UNIVERSITY PRESS
Macon, Georgia
1979–2019
40 Years of Publishing Excellence

MUP/ P580

Published by Mercer University Press
1501 Mercer University Drive
Macon, Georgia 31207

9 8 7 6 5 4 3 2 1

Books published by Mercer University Press are printed on acid-free paper that meets the requirements of the American National Standard for Information Sciences—Permanence of Paper for Printed Library Materials.

Printed and bound in Canada.

This book is set in Adobe Caslon Pro.

ISBN 978-0-88146-701-7

Cataloging-in-Publication Data is available from the Library of Congress

Acknowledgments

America: "I Know a Man."

The American Jounral of Poetry: Vol. Xii "Conversation" and "Grasped by God."

Belletrist: "Poupette (Parts I and II)."

Beltway Poetry Journal: "Lake Rosseau, Canada."

Caprice 32: "A Wedding Song for Ann."

Connotations: "Your Autobiography."

Dan River Review: "Stalking the Reactionary Cleric."

The Hartskill Review: "Message from an Unknown Woman."

The James Dickey Review: "Poetry at the Assisted Living Residence" and "The Human Condition."

Literary Matters: "Boy in Syria" and "The Numbers."

New Letters: "A Harder Art," "PTSD" and "That Boy 2016."

Peacock Journal: "Approaching the Indefinable," "Creativity In The Open Air," "Looking For God, with a line by Richard Wilbur," and "The Intellectus."

Pembroke: "Confessional Poetry."

Tar River Poetry: "Forsaken."

Thinking Continental: "The Burden of Theology."

Tiferet: "On Reading Bonhoeffer" and "The Bible."

Windhover: "On the Relation of the One to the Many."

"Skinning the Ego" was first published in *First Light: A Festschrift for Philip Levine on His 85th Birthday*. Ed. Christopher Buckley. CA: The Press at California State University, Fresno & Greenhouse Review Press, 2013.

My translation of "The Fortunes of Men" first appeared in *The Word Exchange: Contemporary Poets Translate Anglo-Saxon Poems.* Ed. Greg Delanty. Norton, 2010.

Contents

YOUR AUTOBIOGRAPHY

Poems

I.

THE LARGER SENSE OF THINGS

Your Autobiography

By increments, and barely noticeable,
it happens to, around, in, and because
of you—your autobiography, the shadow
you cast upon the earth on which you walk,
writing your life. The story of childhood—
in equal measures surprise and humiliation,
though sometimes there's a glowing Christmas tree
or candles on a cake—segues seamlessly
into the unoriginal years-long
tale of adolescent turbulence.

How many years are left to go? Some lives
are short, and some are longer but haunted by
brutalism: the shadow knows. And all
arrive at a necessary end with the death
of the author, that wrong-headed theory that confuses
life with art. There are no epilogues,
no drafts, no revisions. Your autobiography
concludes as it began, the last page blank.

Confessional Poetry

Once I was wild with loneliness.
Nothing sufficed. I was ready to die.
I do not say this to confess

so much as to acknowledge those
whose friendship I was rescued by.
Once I was wild with loneliness,

and night was a solitary place,
a cell where one could only cry.
I do not say this to confess

nor to broker a separate peace;
rather, because no longer am I,
as I was, wild with loneliness,

enclosed and locked in self. I guess
she's gone, that girl of sorrow and sigh.
I do not say this to confess.

Instead I celebrate the loss
of such constricting agony.
Once I was wild with loneliness.
I say that not to confess.

My Dynamo Family

All gone. The lot of them. Vanished. Vanquished.
My dynamo family. My witty, troubled,
sometimes vicious family, passionate
and brilliant, birthday candles that blew themselves out.

Or shall I revise? Say a hard-luck family
of failures, favors out of reach, too high
to knock down even with a piñata pole.
The disappointment took a murderous toll.

Or were they like a million other families,
captive to a shared yet separate existence
ghosted with secrets and scars and memories
that seldom matched, cross-purposed as they were.

What can one say? There is no way to know
the truth. There is no test a doctor gives
to verify his hunch about your dear
departed. One is stuck with what one makes

of one's personal history. I'll call them mine
but set them aside, out of mind, and in
the hardest, coldest ground, where mystery
regerminates and love and life rebound.

On the Relation of the One to the Many

Everything was the same.
Everywhere one turned, one met the same faces.
Always, the same people doing
the same thing. We called this history,
This sameness,
for it was recordable and endlessly repeatable,
unlike that singular moment
when a certain figure
stepped forward, out of shadow,
and one could see
that here was a self,
of whatever color, sex, shape, tendencies, preferences, citizenship,
different from all others
except oneself.

A Man

I know a man who
knew a man who
as a boy
sat in the front row
in class. The nun who
taught the class
kept on her desk
a wooden crucifix
and a box
of thorns.
Any kid who
misbehaved
had to walk
up to her desk,
take a thorn
from the box and drill
it into the crown
circling Jesus' bent head.
Sin, she said, hurts God.
If you knew the boy who
became the man who
knew the man
I knew,
would you not hold him
in your arms for
a long time,
maybe
forever?

The Human Condition

We stand before the court, accused of treason.
We are accountable. It was our fault,
the killing, raping, water-boarding, all

the crimes, the crimes, the crimes, the crimes, the crimes
against humanity (the poor, the starving,
neglected and malnourished children, the mad,

the uncomprehending, the merely befuddled).
Though it may be invisible, blame
attaches to us like an unfortunate odor.

The Chief Magistrate has taken her seat.
A window that will not quite close admits
a chilling wind. The players are in position.

To whom can we turn? Is there anyone
whom we have not offended?

No. No one.

Skinning the Ego

Levine's enduring collection *News of the World*
curates stories about his friends and family
or maybe just a guy he met somewhere,
sometime. After all, he's just a guy
himself, and guys are everywhere. *Guys and*
Dolls, said Damon Runyon. Phil Levine's poems
circumambulate among memories,
though who can guess what may not be history,
may be a fillip rather than a Philip,
may be imagined or transformed or borrowed.
A master poet, especially a guy,
marks his territory, Siberia
to cities west to California and back.

I've done a bit of traveling myself—
Russia when it was the Soviet Union,
Latvia, the Philippines, Poland,
and elsewhere. There is always a lot of elsewhere.
I've seen the faces of Levine's uncles,
just not on those particular stubborn men.
And married one once. His passions outran his mind,
which was fast but not fast enough to curb
the anger that drove him to a kind of wildness.
I like the way the poems in *News of the World*
travel beyond the poet's self to gain
perspective, that under-recognized virtue
that seems to threaten our felicity

and peace of mind, as if peace of mind
were possible without it. Then I met
Levine. We'd met before, on a staircase

in Minneapolis. He hadn't remembered
but why would he? This time we met in Chicago.
A conference. A gathering of writers.
He shared the stage with Carol Ann Duffy, Poet
Laureate of Britain. He was now Poet
Laureate of the United States. And I
was Poet Laureate of Virginia and sat
next to him until he was called on stage. Our sitting
next to each other was purely accidental;
I had no part to play in this scene, was but

a spectator. Someone along for the drive, the moment.
The two were good together. Repartee
made laughter bloom in the big, crowded room.
I laughed as hard as anyone there. The poets
could have been a vaudeville team, doing
stand-up shtick. Okay, I thought, there are
ways and ways to skin the savage ego.
There are ways and ways to keep things in perspective.
So why is it so hard, humility?
Humility without humiliation.
One does not entail the other, nor
are ourselves deserving of much notice,
but notice, should it come, can be deflected

by the larger sense of things, the living, the dead.

A Harder Art

cf. *Elizabeth Bishop*, "One Art"

Harder to master than the art of losing,
the art of forgiveness requires a sacrifice
of ego, a deliberate and painful choosing

of other over self. Accept the bruising
of faults disclosed (your every little vice).
Harder to master than the art of losing,

to forgive's to give, one writes, meanwhile musing
on one's failed attempts to be normal and nice,
to subdue the stubborn, selfish self, choosing

other over self. How very confusing.
I can't deny that I have paid a price,
grace being harder to master than the art of losing.

I thought I was the Queen of Sheba, lazing
on a silken couch, or maybe just a niece
of the Queen but still among the specially chosen.

How wrong I was. I might have started boozing
or using, moved to Barcelona or Nice.
Harder to master than the art of losing,
the art of forgiving is an act of choosing.

Poetry at the Assisted Living Residence

They break my heart when they die, and die
they do. I think of Annie, her mind still clear,
whose penciled poems remembered growing up
on her father's farm, the Osage orange aflame
in morning light, the baler bundling hay,
the stray kitten she befriended who kept
the mice at bay or at least in the barn.
And just last week Bertie nearly died
but fought her way back here from whatever it is
they see—a tunnel, light, their parents, perhaps,
or Jesus clad in a cloud-white robe like those
terry-cloth ones better hotels supply.
Bertie'd already had a disabling stroke
and couldn't speak but listened with her whole
body. Ashes to ashes, we say, without
considering the fact very closely.
Ashes to ashes, we say, and ministers
say it, and what we like about it is
the way it glosses over the body in
decay, the way it skips the months and days
of failing organs and dysfunctional functions,
the pain and messiness before the death
and the stink and falling flesh afterward.
I wish the wasting did not suffer, though
I know they do. I hope that fear does not
overtake them on their final journey,
though I cannot imagine that it won't.
It isn't easy to accustom oneself
to students who, instead of dropping out,
die. May they never know no transformation
came to their rescue, never know they drowned

in the swirling River of Lethe, their bones picked clean by fish nibbling
endlessly, their reminiscent
poems and themselves as gone as gone can be.

Twenty-one Coptic Christians

When ISIL force-marched Coptic Christians to
the edge of Libya and made them kneel
on the shore of the fabled Mediterranean sea
and divested them of their heads one by one
the sea ran red as if it had been changed
to wine but wine the sea was sickeningly not.
Who can explain the horror of that day?
Not I, nor you. Nor any God we may
invent. Our world is rife with murderers:
that's how it is. And yet this very morning
I learned a hermit thrush, his feathers puffed
against the biting cold, has got a crush
on my lovely husband, tagging along beside—
six feet away—on walks through peaceful woods.

Message From an Unknown Woman

They invaded the fields
hid in shadows in the streets
cut our husbands' throats
They say they are going to burn the children
They say the children will go up in flames
like bonfires, but we think it will be
a long baking, our children turning charcoal, then ashen.
My mother has been raped at eighty
My sister lies down so a man can piss on her
The pantry is bare, the milk sour
My children cling to my skirt like flies
            and I have to sweep them off,
my beautiful children who never speak,
my children who do not play beneath the baobab.

The Catalogue of Injury

The catalogue of injury done to man
by man outstrips the measure of man's mind.
Here, "man" includes "women." Think of Tashfeen
Malik or the unnatural nurse at Ravensbrück
who slipped cyanide into her patients' throats
(O dry as the Sahara). The catalogue
of injury abbreviates nothing,
neither the physical nor the mental.
Neither the recipient nor the injurer.
Nor the injury the injurer does to himself
or herself, she who said she floated through
falling snow at night in Moscow to
Prokofiev. And were there spies? Informers?
Were there prisoners caged in unseen cells?
There were. But what could she have done for them?
People endure every kind of hardship
or they don't, and then the concert ends.

II

WAR AND ESPIONAGE

Dicks

I. STALKING THE REACTIONARY CLERIC

In Hungary, the dreaded secret police
disguised themselves as monks, Franciscan robes
flowing over trousers like muddy rivers.
Reactionary clerics were what they stalked,
and if they found them they were sent straightway
to the Gulag. If not, they sent whomever balked.

II. THE THIRD BERLIN FESTIVAL, 1951

The Stasi served as drivers, caterers
and organizers, all the better to keep
their eyes on *West* Berlin participants;
they called this Operation Sunrise, this
surveillance of the competition, this
undercover recruitment of foreign spies.
Everywhere, eyes snooped on eyes. Dicks
tripped over dicks. A grand time was had
by almost all (of the dicks, anyway).

III. RUSSIAN SPIES IN POLAND

Russian spies in Poland spoke impeccable
Polish, were fans of art and theatre,
imbibed the finest of French wines, and lured
lovers of Chopin to intimate soirées
whereat they handcuffed poets and pianists.

IV. IN LENINGRAD, 1975

Babes in the woods they were, those Russian teens
clustered at a table next to ours. They'd pushed
their way into the restaurant to eavesdrop
on our small group. *They steal, or break some law,*
and then they are in hock to the secret police,
my friend explained. They craned their necks to hear
what he was saying. They were baby dicks,
not yet matured, not yet aware that poison
was circulating through their eager veins.

The Burden of Theology

It was the burden of theology
to reconcile human love with death
but now theology has failed to do
what it was meant to do and in its place
we have the nihilism of savagery,
the cynicism of the ruthless rich,
the flagrant brutalization of girls and women,
a planet hopelessly in disrepair.

What can we do? Not turn back. The past
is past and irredeemable, a river
racing downstream, white water rapids none
can navigate. The former gods are old
and tired, they walk with canes, their backs hunched,
their eyesight fading, hearing failing, knees
like ladders that collapsed when we weren't looking.
Nor are there new ones who will rescue us.

I do not mean that we can stand in for
the gods of yesterday. I mean that all
of us together can make a difference
no god could or would make. But trust is necessary
to re-envision human life, and trust
is what we lack. So are we doomed to die
and die out? It seems so. We must not fool ourselves.
The future's here. It will not last for long.

Female Snipers

For obvious reasons, it's hard to praise a sniper.
The people killed. That they are killed from far
away. That often the sniper is hard to spot,
or at a safe distance. But snipers come in handy
when war arrives, and war arrives with some
frequency.
    Female snipers excelled.
Lyudmila, Roza, and Violette,
for example.

1.

        When Germany invaded
the Soviet Union, Lyudmila racked up
well over three hundred kills, including enemy
snipers. She lugged a semi-automatic.
Before the war, she studied history.
After it, she worked as a historian.
In between, she toured America,
Canada, and England, dazzling crowds.
Two stamps celebrated her lovely face.
Woody Guthrie wrote a song in her honor.
But what do we know now of who she was?
She refused to be a nurse. She was brave.
And she found American journalists rude, wanting
her skirt to be as short as American skirts.

2.

In battlefields where blood ran dark as Hades
Roza Shanina was a spark of light.
There is no doubt she knocked some eyeballs back.
She had no trouble filling out the khaki shirt—
regulation issue—and blue wool skirt,
her sunny hair a most unmartial flag.
Barely eighteen but confident, she awed
the male contingent not only with her breasts
but also by the precision with which she took out
moving targets, often two in a row.
The men were relieved to have her on their side
and made their appreciation known.
                                        Roza
liked kids. If she could not afford university
when war was over—tuition had climbed—she wanted
to run a home for orphans. Little ones would laugh
at the funny faces she pulled and she'd have hugged
the shy, who learned at such an early age
that living in the world is hard and war
is even worse. She kept a combat diary
and could have been a writer but was dead
at twenty. The River Lethe is deeper than deep
and swallows the whole of human history.

3.

Violette was something of a wild child,
a mischief maker, dark-haired, small, and bold.

Even grown up she was in favor of fun.
It was her father who taught her to handle a gun.

She married a man she'd known for forty-two days,
Étienne Szabo. She met him on Bastille Day.

His ancestry was Hungarian.
Chest wounds killed him at El Alamein.

He never had a chance to see his daughter.
His wife took his place as a dedicated fighter.

Escape, evasion, and other tricks of the trade
became secondhand. Plans and traps were laid.

A gunfight in Vichy France had her killing
Nazis and spitting fire. No way was she willing

to cooperate with men who took from her
her husband. Interrogation and torture

ensued. The Nazis sent her to the concentration
camp Ravensbrück, where, daily, evil was done.

Told to kneel, and shot in the back of her head,
she was twenty-three. Twenty-three and dead.

She was one of those who tried to help other
captives in the camp with a word, or smudge of butter.

Stalingrad, November 1942

Imagine that on this page is printed a poem
about the Battle of Stalingrad. Imagine
the men—and strong-souled women—who fought and died,
their brains blown out, their corpses in rigor mortis.
We must imagine, because no one can show it to us.
No one can show us that sky the color of steel.
No one can show us the pregnant women with rifles,
the Russian men in their belted greatcoats, skirts flaring.
No one can show us the burned-out, falling buildings,
the gutted houses, the desolate, undone infrastructure,
the animals whose misfortune it was to be there then.
No one can show us the stink and slosh of battle,
the flushed faces of the men, children crying.
War is a map of what does not exist.

Stalingrad, November 1942 (II)

A newly posted soldier might live for most of a day.
A squadron commander, and experienced officer, three days.

They knew that if they did not fight they would die.
That if they did fight they would die.
That if they fled they would be caught and executed.

Stalingrad was a morgue without walls
or a roof or a floor.

There was no shortage of corpses.

The Numbers

The numbers make no sense. We have to start
with one. One Jew. One Communist. One Pole
or homosexual or gypsy or sick
or physically or mentally challenged citizen.
Or sometimes two, as in the case of twins
subjected to experiments no sane
experimenter could conceive. And then
the numbers begin to multiply: Jehovah's
Witnesses, political dissenters,
every one who got in the way of a Nazi,
the Nazis being, of course, everywhere.

Sure, we've tried to add the numbers up
but always someone is missing, the infant slung
against an electric fence, the child who walked
away from a forced march but died of the cold
in a barn or field. *You* try adding them up.

We cannot.

And what about the hard-working prostitute
who struggled to protect her daughter from
the men who'd stroke her fine-haired arm or pat
her on the head and run their hands farther
down her still-flat chest? The girl was eight.

We have to start with that *one*. Anyone.
Anyone and everyone, remembering
that someone is always among the many missing.

Simone ("Poupette") Alizon

1

Poupette was no coquette,
no French flirt.

At seventeen she pedaled her *velo* from
one end of Paris to the farther other,

delivering news of the Résistance to
the Résistance.

Brave, yes. Foolish?
Perhaps not—

A pretty girl who smiles defers suspicion
at least for a little while.

In her bike basket, a baguette,
aroma more seductive than Chanel,
Poupette herself as fresh and new and warm.

Of course they caught her.
The Vichy police were everywhere,
the Résistance only here and there.

Clandestine photographs confirmed her lawlessness.

The eight months she spent in solitary
she longed for her older sister, who longed for her.

2

In time both girls were sent to Birkenau
and each rejoiced to see her dear sister.

But soon disease made Marie's legs swell up
so much that she became unable to walk.

Now Marie relied on her younger sister.
Maybe, said Marie, *we didn't pray*

enough.
        Can anyone ever pray enough?

The ground fog in tatters as if shreds had been strewn
around, and sometimes a shred corkscrewed upward

until it fell again.... Sometimes the sun
broke through to gild the peeling birches whose

branches cut like whips.... Marie's red lips
turned black as midnight and lice colonized

her still body. Poupette was now alone.
After the war, she married and had children

but nothing ever made her happy again.
She had not prayed enough though she had prayed

day after day after day after day.

In the Tent at Ravensbrück, Himmler's Concentration Camp for Women

I try to see myself in this place where babies were born and died overnight, frozen into tiny statues. I smell the stink. I hear the mothers wail when infants are yanked from their bone-dry breasts. I cross my arms against the furious cold. And my child? Do I have a child? But even imagining, I cannot bring myself to insert a child here. Somewhere else, perhaps. Not here. Worse than a scene in Dante's hell: the noise, the dead babies, the tent so crammed you'd have thought it a city of the damned.

In the Hospital at Ravensbrück

What species of doctor would remove a healthy woman's collar bone or cut deep into a leg, pack it with glass and dirt, and wait for infection to take hold? *Rabbits*, the women were called. What madness was this? The inability to understand that all earth's creatures love their too-short lives? Or hatred so deep that cutting it out needed knives?

Night of the Murdered Poets

Not all were poets but all were Jews.
The official phrase was "rootless cosmopolitans."
Stalin's madness had mushroomed, criminal murder
magnified by hysteria. A madness
poisonous as toxic mushrooms like
destroying angel, *death cap*, and *deadly dapperling*.

A secret trial. No defending lawyers
nor even any prosecutors. *Trial?*
Three military judges, who requested
clarification of synagogues and
kosher food. The leading judge sought permission
to begin again because so much was wrong.

He was not eager to execute the prisoners
but Stalin was. No information about
the trial appeared anywhere. Relatives
were exiled in 1952. Three years
later, they learned the miserable truth: A review
uncovered "no substance to the charges."

WMD

Now you see them.
Now you don't.

The top hat holds
pink-nosed bunnies.

The sleeve is stuffed
with Persian scarves.

But where are the weapons
of mass destruction?

Hidden, says Cheney.
Hidden, says Bush.

Camouflage, say both.
Shock and awe, they say.

Oh sure, why not start a war?
After all, everybody dies someday.

P.T.S.D.

We were hunkered down behind enemy lines,
wearing Woodland, with leaves atop our heads,
inching nearer kingdom come. The sun at noon
made us itch in our mud-encrusted fatigues.

Bees hummed, locusts shrilled, mosquitoes
dive-bombed. The sun moved not an inch.
We were in the time before time ended,
waiting for the gun, the knife, the grenade

or bomb. People say: What was it like
over there? *It was like waiting for the end*
of the world. They say, You're home now.
Maybe. But we're still waiting.

Wounded Warrior

His wife's eyes slide away from him
because she is sick with shock.
He does not blame her.
The man in the mirror is not who he was.

The children are afraid of him
and approach cautiously.
He does not blame them.
The man in the mirror is a monster.

The dog wants to lick his human's wounds,
nuzzle the missing limbs.
The wounded warrior
shuns the mirror like ostracism.

Boy in Syria

A child should be the future, not the past.

Six…Eight at most.
His face a flower beginning to bloom.
A boy beginning to wake to truth.

The truth in this place is sarin gas.
It paralyzes the diaphragm,

is a nerve agent that makes it impossible for people to breathe.

They tear off their clothes.
They claw at the air.
They are being strangled by something they cannot see.

The struggle wrenches them into grotesque positions
like origami.

The soul watches in disbelief
as body is stripped from it.

The boy had plans.
He was going to be a lawyer or doctor.
He was going to play soccer on Sunday.

Protest in Budapest, July 20, 2014

The black eagle representing evil,
its beak a knife, talons stretched out to grip,
plunges in perpetuity to seize
the angel Gabriel, traditional protector
of Hungary: this is a description
of the newest monument in Liberty Square,
visible from our hotel window. The
monument divides Hungarians.
Some think it whitewashes history
(meaning collaboration with the Nazis).
Protesters bring photographs of murdered Jews,
bring a grandfather's shoes, or suitcase left behind,
knickknacks and tochkas, an antediluvian typewriter,
and narratives of loss and bitter heartbreak.
Police wear red berets but do not seek
to limit freedom of expression: this
is a "peaceful" protest, so peaceful the protest is
marginalized, sun radiating warmth,
kids dashing in and out of the splashing fountains
that rim the perimeter. If Hungarians
cannot agree for whom the monument
was built, does not the war continue? Have
not the murdered Jews been murdered twice?

Drowned

From Hungary to Austria: we made
that three-hour trip on a comfortable train,
unlike the exhausted thousands walking now
to what they hope is freedom, to what they hope
is a job and a safe place to call their home.
Yet some of these have died already, drowned
in the Mediterranean, the three-year-old,
the five-year-old, their mother swallowed up
in dark-blue swells, father shocked to find
he's still alive. What can he do? Nothing
that is not shadowed by memory, blue chains
that bind him to the darkest grotto. Ghosts
of prehistoric crocodiles ever
accompany his search for those lost lives.

Concerning the Dead

We know the dead are unaware they're dead.
They may have known they were about to be,
but no escaped soul or fragment of soul
or consciousness exists any longer.
In this, there is a kind of comfort though
it's not the kind of paradisal afterlife
once offered. It's a comfort only to
the not-yet-dead, not to the already dead,

except for those whose bodies are delivered
free of their reasoning heads, those summits of
intelligence believed to hold a thought
or two or a perception or first line
of a poem up perhaps to twelve seconds.
Twelve lo-o-o-ng seconds. I like to think they were not
thinking so much as looking at the crowd,
the silver sea, or sky as sheer as glass

and the widest window in the world, but thought
or observation held will not hold when capitals
are separated, toppling from human columns.
Of course architecture's a euphemism here
for an ugly way to die and the widest window's
not the sky: it is the awful gap in the neck,
the throat's sputtering gurgle, the deconstruction
of meaningful life to meaningless death, utter

eradication of the soul's local genius.

THAT BOY 2016

Halfway around the world, that boy who wore
blood in his hair and sat obligingly
because he could not comprehend Assad's
reign of evil is, I now believe,
the son I would have had, if only I
were younger and if only I could have
had a child and if he did not belong
already to a family in Aleppo.

I too can't comprehend Assad's black reign
of evil. Does it cheer him up to fling
small boys into a cauldron of hurtling fire?
I think it must. Yet all a little boy
wants is a toy or two and his parents
and if he has a sibling, then he wants
his sibling. Pita bread would also be
good, but there is no pita bread.

III

DIALOGUES WITH DIETRICH BONHOEFFER

On Reading Bonhoeffer

One may decide he was delusional.
How else could he believe in Paradise?
An island in the sky with easy breezes,
with California palms and descant angels,
a place that isn't anywhere unless
it's going to turn up in a fifth dimension.

(Or twenty-fifth, considering string theory.)
His father and a brother were agnostic
scientists but had no evidence
that God did not exist. Nor can there be
a proof of what is not, although the odds
of God existing shrink from year to year.

Thus, they've shrunk since the German pastor believed
but plenty of theologians even then
did not consider Christ divine. Yet Dietrich
thought we should be disciples of the Lord
in all respects and trained himself as one,
and he was brave and kind and logical.

But then again if premises are false
the argument, however logical,
must plummet into disrepute, and yet
again, the German pastor surely knew
this, so I ask again, How could the man
believe? I think it is a mystery,

the kind of mystery no one can solve,
the kind of mystery that's close to miracle,
the kind of mystery the stars bespeak,

the kind of mystery clear skies disguise,
the kind of mystery our hearts take to heart.

First Conversation

"Nothing is so at odds with prayer as vanity."—*Dietrich Bonhoeffer*

Yet vanity entraps us, not in mirrors
or reflections or even giddy praise
but in the steps we take to prove ourselves
not vain, not prideful, neither self-obsessed
nor falsely humble. In fact, the farther down
we dig, the deeper strata we expose,
including layer on layer of self-deception,
which tends to mislead others, not just ourselves.

I don't object to what the preacher says.
I only say it's hard as hell to do.

Grasped by God

"Grasped by God"—*Dietrich Bonhoeffer*

But if we don't believe there is a God,
we will not find ourselves grasped by God.

Unless perhaps we've taken notice of
life's defenselessness against the scythe

that threshes us all as if we're wheat or grass.
The poet Plath described electric shock

as being grasped by a God who held her by
the roots of her hair—her permed, peroxided hair.

I don't think *that* God was a God either.
I do think there are paths that we are called

to take, if not by God, by love, and don't
we like to say that God is love?

The Bible

"For the first time I discovered the Bible."—*Dietrich Bonhoeffer*

To him it was the word of God.
Reading the word, he heard the word.
Hearing the word, he abided by it.
Abiding by the word, he drew close
to Christ as if the Christ were present
now and for evermore. We live
in Time? But Bonhoeffer lived in Christ—
Christ being all time, as God may be
thought of as eternity.
His Christ was no abstraction, was
eternity revealed in time.
The crackling storm, the cheerful meadow
refreshed, the blowing tops of trees
take place in time but speak to us
of centuries of life on earth.
How could the German pastor trust
his Christ would not evaporate?
A twisted freak of wind—and Christ
might fly like leaves before a storm
or die, like drafts before a poem.
And didn't Christ die once? Why not
again, should God insist upon it.
The temporal is always agitated;
the nature of eternity is calm—
a calm that steadies and revives.
Daily the pastor meditated
on verses complex and meaningful
but how could he believe in what
he read? How could he live his life

according to what someone else
proposed? *Discipleship*, he said:
The perfect man was Christ, therefore
the man still unperfected must
observe and follow the perfected one.

The Christ

> "The figure of the Crucified invalidates all thought which takes success for its standard."—*Dietrich Bonhoeffer*

This I accept, for Christ, I think, is not
the mortal Jesus but a lasting concept
or icon or meme inhabiting the nexus
of joy and sorrow, love and loss of love.

The mortal Jesus—one of countless humans
taken into custody, tried, sentenced—
tortured—murdered—was unremarkable.
It's true that he was oddly charismatic,

but in every other respect he was one of us.
Like all of us, he was at the mercy of
his finite body, its physical properties,
the need to feed, to clean, to clothe its parts.

As for the mind—he thought in parables,
nor was this uncommon in biblical Judea.
The mind has always favored stories over
the careful logic of philosophy.

And yet philosophy is what great minds
become. Not just philosophical but
philosophy; the thought becomes the thing
as does the artist's art, the poet's song,

the master composer's daring composition.
Small wonder then that Christ transcends time.

He is the meaning of himself, the good
news—*and, Dietrich, the bad*: there is no God,

only the suffering Christ, and he is all of us.

In the American South

> "The way the Southerners talk about the negroes is simply repugnant, and in this regard the pastors are no better than the others."
> — *Dietrich Bonhoeffer*

This most certainly was true. It's true
today, nearly ninety years on, a hardened
resentful bitterness that blinds so many
to their suffering brethren. Probably not the pastors.
And not as many as once there were, but quite
enough to tarnish pewter skies, albino
sun at noon, the Carolina coast.
Something sordid haunts our habitat still
and not only at night but on Sundays,
false fellow-feeling negating the truth, requisite
compassion distorted by sentimental homilies.

In New York

The Harlem Renaissance was underway.
He preached at Abyssinian Baptist, invited
by Adam Clayton Powell, and here at last
beheld the community of joy he'd hoped
to find. Americans introduced him to
the social agencies that sought to help
all those with hearts aching to be touched by
kindness. The pastor, still with morning dew
upon his forehead, understood that what
theology needed was a grounding in
the black-and-white realities of life.

Hans Memling's *Head of Christ*, Which Bonhoeffer Viewed at the Metropolitan Museum of Art

The eyes are larger than life,
his hair in separated ringlets,
brows and fine nose echoing
the length of his brown hair.
His mouth is as small as a girl's,
lips full but tidily restrained,
skimpy beard a shadow or stain.

The eyes stare back at the viewer.
It's hard to read those eyes
because they seem to read us.
Bonhoeffer may have sensed
a message or commandment in
the portrait. Not literally,
but those eyes interrogate.

The dignity of this head of Christ
asks us to do what is right.
To be responsible.
Bonhoeffer knew what *he*
was responsible for: ridding
Germany of the Fuhrer.
Satan. Lucifer. The goddamn Devil.

Making Up His Mind (Second trip to the U.S.,1939)

"In the evening thousands of fire-flies in the garden, like flying fire."
—*Dietrich Bonhoeffer*

He called it *flying fire*—the thousands of fireflies
celebrating oncoming night in Lakeville,
Connecticut. It was nineteen-thirty-nine
and he was homesick for *Deutschland,* his faithful friends
and family. If he did not return
to Berlin, he thought, he'd be not a pastor
but an impostor, a churchman who'd abandoned
his sheep in the lurch. It had been a mistake to come
again to America; he had a sense,
peculiar as it was, that the future was following
him, that one of the infamous trio of Fates
had caught him up, her cadaverous bony arm
outstretched and searching for his pasty neck.
As twilight deepened into dark and dark
was dressed in dew, the dancing fire grew still
and stars usurped the sky. *What should I do,*
he asked himself although he already knew
the consequential course he had to take:
Return to Germany. Defy the tyrant.

Stallion

> "Where God tears great gaps we should not try to fill them with human words. They should remain open."—*Dietrich Bonhoeffer*

Which is to say, I think, that horror won't
be gentled. Horror, with its wide, frantic eyes
and wild gyrations, cannot be soothed or calmed
nor should it be, as that would be a lie.
See, now, the creature standing on hind legs,
its front hoofs tearing at invisible air.
Massive and frightened, it may hurt itself.
The creature's heart may blow like a tire.
Survivors will burn the carcass.

What We Owe the Innocent

"[B]andage the victims under the wheel, but jam the spoke in the wheel itself."—*Dietrich Bonhoeffer*

The very moment Nazis rose to power
our wet-behind-the-ears beardless pastor
warned Germany against idolatry,
the idol with clay feet being Adolf Hitler.
Help those who cannot help themselves, he said,
but fight the criminals who stole the state.

And what of the stable in the Tiergarten
that in 1945 burned down,
horses racing down the Kurfűrstendamm,
their manes aflame, their streaming tails like rivers on fire,
the great throats screaming.

Who can ignore the death cries of the innocent?

The Living Truth

To find "the Living Truth," Bonhoeffer said,
one must be in relation to the Christ:
a declaration brave and dangerous
at a time when Adolf Hitler thought *he* was God.

A person in relation to the Christ
was in a conversation with the Christ.

Thus were the Ten Commandments demoted to
self-help, although the person was required
to search his motives, pray, and read scripture.
So he did and ended up in prison.

A personal relationship with God?
That immaterial, ineffable construct
devised to save us from our loneliness,
our losses, all the pain that we endure?

God is a phantom, flickering like a firefly.
How could one ever know that it was real,
that personal relationship with God?
Because revelation is a matter of belief,

or as the church, any church, would say,
faith. "Living" suggests the resurrected Christ,
of course. But what is faith?
A whisper in the wind.

Death and Redemption

> "Death reveals that the world is not as it should be but that it stands in need of redemption. Christ alone is the conquering of death."
> —*Dietrich Bonhoeffer*

Beautiful words well ordered and in his time
they may have made sense, if not altogether truth,
but now we average adults know more:
how black holes consume light and light bends handily
like a hillside sapling tossed in a sprightly wind.

We hear of weak and strong anthropic principles
and of ingenious questions we never knew
would need answering. Of dark energy.
Thus death no longer is the one sure thing
exposing wrongness in our lovely world.

Consider the expanding universe,
the particles that should be somewhere but
so far are not. Prophesied tachyons.
The Singlet boson. Warps in time. How far
away from God are we this very day?

It's true we need redemption for our sins,
our many, many sins and shortcomings,
but there's no god anywhere to provide
redemption or to wipe clean our crowded slates.
We have to make amends as best we can.

And don't expect a prize. Paradise
does not await. No one will congratulate
the sinner for his reformation or

her lame attempts to apologize. We judge
ourselves and find ourselves wanting. This is knowledge
we must live with as long as we shall live.

Abstract Concepts

"All concepts of reality that ignore Jesus Christ are abstractions."
—*Dietrich Bonhoeffer*

Agreed: that all such concepts are abstractions.
But this does not mean Jesus Christ himself's

not an abstraction—or say a finicky wind
slow dancing with linden trees and swallowtails.

His human form's defunct and what we feel
is not his holy presence but the weight

of all the feeling we pour into him,
as if he were the very well at Cana

from which he drew the wedding wine. Surely
we do not think he waits at heaven's gate

to welcome us to bliss? Would that he did.
Instead, the weather's hot or cold and either

way we die. Knowing this does not negate
kindness, clarity, or charity,

all of which are real as realization.

Heresy

> "[T]here should be a shot of heresy in every good sermon."
> —*Dietrich Bonhoeffer to Wolf-Dieter Zimmermann*

A shot of heresy
is necessary
to poke the congregation,
slumping, awake. A shot
with a sting like whisky or vodka.
A shot that snaps back the necks
of the flock and flares the eyes
and nostrils. A shot like a Glock.
A shot at a basket or goalie.
A shot like a game of billiards.
A shot at winning. A shot
like amphetamine, the needle in
the addict's arm. A shot
like a finely honed crack. A shot
like the first of World War One.

The Center

"A violation of the Gospel"—*Dietrich Bonhoeffer*

The center, the German pastor insisted, is Christ.
To Adolf Hitler, this was blasphemy
as he considered himself the one true god
and wasn't he proving it by his actions, which
included killing the helpless, locking up
the argumentative, casting out
—well, anyone he wished, including Jews?
Our pastor fled to parishes in London.
There he could at least refer to Jesus
Christ and the Chosen, the Children of Israel.

How could Christianity deny
the legacy of Moses? the Psalms? the prophets?
To be a Christian was to be beholden
to the Jews, he said. But maybe that was why,
exactly why, the Reich Church decided
that Jews should wander in the wilderness
once again toughing things out with manna.

Joy and Sorrow

> "In recent years we have really learnt how much joy and sorrow can and must fill the human heart at one and the same time."—*Dietrich Bonhoeffer*

The recent years had been a feverish contagion
of lies and murder, language a black veil meant
to hide the base features of Hitler's heart:
hatred, contempt, inability
to understand that others weren't so empty
as himself, his frenzied plans to make
himself a god,or at least a Caesar. Kaiser.
Yes, well, a god.
The pastor kept abreast of news.
His students had been killed in war or jailed
as pacifists. Colleagues had been martyred.
He lived in a vise of anguish yet read his Bible,
Overjoyed by what he found therein.

He did not simplify what is complicated.

Thrushes

"Here in the prison yard there is a thrush which sings beautifully in the morning, and now in the evening too."—*Dietrich Bonhoeffer*

My father once composed an anthem to
"The Darkling Thrush" by Thomas Hardy. How
he loved that poem. It spoke to him the way
another thrush had spoken to the pastor
in his prison, morning and night. Bonhoeffer expressed
his great gratitude for the simplest things
and I feel called upon to join with him
in praise of much such:
The way the sun guides us
through the usual day.
How darkness gathers
on the chairs and couch
in a room where friends engage
in pleasant talk.
  The sleeping dog.
The stars
come out on their broad boardwalk of sky
to keep watch.
   Hibiscus opening when sunlight returns,
a drastic change surprising no one and yet
surprising us from one day to the next.
The day that Hardy heard the darkling thrush—
a played-out bird, almost, it seemed, as old
as the century ending but still appreciative
of life and song—he wondered a creature so close
to death could still rejoice. What hope sustained
its simple song? He did not know, but hope
there was and it heartened Thomas Hardy.

Creativity in the Open Air

> "...the *hilaritas—'cheerfulness'*—which is to be found in any really great and free intellectual achievement."—*Dietrich Bonhoeffer*

He learned the importance of not being earnest
from Beethoven, Bach, Mozart, Goethe, Schiller
but did he think the artist manufactures
blithe comedy for the sake of an audience?
Never. He understood *hilaritas* springs
from *gravitas*, the artist's hard-won command
of tools and technology, even when
technology is punctuation. Art
releases artist into freedom, where
the master can play, explore, design, and shape
her capabilities as she will—and won't
she laugh for the fun of it, the fun of work?

The air the artist breathes uplifts like prayer,
supporting the mythical kingdom in the sky.

Simplicity

"Simplicity is an intellectual achievement, one of the greatest."—*Dietrich Bonhoeffer*

Simplicity's foundational, groundwork
before the many flourishes subtle
or exuberant. Flourishes
include recursion, counterpoint, shifting
keys and arpeggios. The mile-high flock
of notes in Beethoven's last piano sonata,
in the last movement (there are only two),
transforms our mundane lives to piercing beauty,
unequalled beauty that mirrors both life and death.
A theme must be reduced to its essence
then complicated into arresting moments,
though such moments need not be loud. That which
is simple transitions to complexity
yet remains strong and clear, the structure sound
as a star that shines for billions of years, dying
long after the death of our own hometown planet.

If

> "...there comes over me a longing (unlike any other that I experience to have a child and not to vanish without a trace...." *Dietrich Bonhoeffer*

He would have doted on a child,
or else have lectured it to death.
The boy or girl, blond as he,
burping, and busting into a smile
sweet as a flounce of baby's-breath,
would hold the father's heart as gently

as the father held the newborn baby.
A father's heart is torn between
his joy and his sudden fear
of the illimitable responsibility he now assumes. Can the child hear
how Father's heart breaks open, keens?

His cry is piercing and oddly wild,
as if he were the newborn child,
and not the child. The mother, mild
as Mary but smarter at mathematics,
allows Father his moment with the child
whom he would teach homiletics.

He transfers the baby to its mother.
His hands were full and now are empty.
For a second he feels wholly bereft,
until he sees his child in Maria's arms
somewhat like the holy family
and becomes aware of love's extraordinary depth.

We Are Part of One

> "…how closely our own lives are bound up with other people's, and in fact how the centre of our own lives is outside ourselves, and how little we are separate entities."—*Dietrich Bonhoeffer*

We are not one, but we are part of one,
for human feeling has a limited range.
Shades aplenty, yes, from subtle to outsized
emotions that besiege us even as velvet
curtains drop and hide the scenes we watched,
Ophelia floating downstream, the salesman's pitch
as life bypasses him. And those are mere
constructions—words and choreography.
The scripted gestures, marks intended to be hit . . .
Their tragedies affect us, make us feel
and think, and feeling and thinking are surely real,
but unhappy Ophelia and the lonely salesman
are not the flesh-and-blood of relatives
or friends or lovers or even enemies,
given the tangle one gets into when
one's bête noir breathes down one's only neck.
Adolf Hitler was Bonhoeffer's bête noir
and yet the German pastor celebrated
the infinite connections that light up
our one world like a string of Christmas lights.
In this, we feel his love and concern
and in return love him.

Guidance

> "...how are we to find the 'Thou' in this 'It' (i.e. fate), or, in other words, how does 'fate' really become guidance?"—*Dietrich Bonhoeffer*

Of course I think that fate is just the when
and where we are. Perhaps we did not mean
to land in this particular place at this
particular point but surely our own actions
have played a role, and maybe all the roles.
We have colluded with ourselves. We have
collaborated with the choices allowed.
We are not innocent. Without a 'Thou'
we must rely upon ourselves, though if
some 'Thou' should speak to us some night we might
think long before turning out the only light.

Polyphony

He called it the polyphony of life,
the way life has of orchestrating themes,
serioso and festive, sad and glad.

Surely one theme of his was Jesus Christ.
Another, the Confessing Church. Third
perhaps his close friendship with Eberhard Bethge.

But there were more: The Old Testament
without which there could not have been the New.
His family. His love of art and music.

Also, he offered, "earthly affection," for which
his referent was the "earthy" Song of Songs.
Thus themes accrue and among them we must find

the German Question: what to do with Hitler?
And what to do with Hitler's thugs and what
to do with all the broken, hopeless people?

A theme with counterpoint will emphasize
not duality but pluralism,
not opposition but coordination,

the fitting in of all the elements
that make the picture whole, that make the union
whole and everlasting, indissoluble.

Looking for God, with a Line by Richard Wilbur

> "We are to find God in what we know, not in what we don't know."—
> *Dietrich Bonhoeffer*

The spectacular advance of science
in his time—and in his family—
did not disturb a pastor who took so
much pleasure in the things of this world.

He loved the warmth of sun on his skin,
"reminding me that I'm a corporeal being."
Eighteen months locked up in Tegal Prison,
he must have felt himself incorporeal,

a man without existence, ghostly as
a candle sputtering out, the wick drowning
in a mini-pool of wax at the candle's base.
A man of no consequence, ineffectual,

he thought, but kept on writing anyway.
When he wrote we'd not find God in what is not
already known, he meant that science is not
where we should look, that God is in the day

and night, the everyday and every night,
the air we breathe, the ground on which we walk,
the flame with which he lit his pipe or smoked
a cigarette, the rain that fell too often

outside his window, where he watched the leaves
changing as the seasons changed. Enjoy
the earth, he said again and again,

and in so many ways. Look for the light,

he would have said as light sank into twilight.
Be alert to birdsong. To the child who will become
a member of the adult human race.
These things we know and in them we find God.

Or he did, though I do confess that while
I do not find God there, I find a world sanctified
by the teachings of Jesus Christ as did the pastor
who prayed to be outside and within it.

Christ's Anguish

At the tail end of a letter, Eberhard Bethge asked him, "What about the anguish of Christ, about which something has to be said?"

Dietrich appears not to have replied to the question
or possibly his letter went astray.
So many did in that time of war, and not
only letters. Manuscripts and books
(reduced to ashes), people and their pets,
wedding rings, apartments, and the bodies—
the bodies, too, reduced to ash or lost
in snow on the Eastern front. One hardly knew
just where one was, so much moving around,
so much scrambled, traded, appropriated.
Yet the question survives: what *about* the anguish of Christ?
We see him drag the heavy wood uphill;
next, see nails hammered through his hands and feet,
the spear in his side, the thieves on either side.
All the backbreaking grief that we endure,
he carries on his own cross-pinned back,
his anguish multiplied by yours and mine,
every fiber of his being weighed down,
his eyes bloodshot, throat dry, the pain so unbearable
he thinks his own father has betrayed him.

Forsaken

"God would have us know that we must live as men who manage our lives without him. The God who is with us is the God who forsakes us."—*Dietrich Bonhoeffer*

That this is what God wants I do not doubt
although I doubt that there's a God who wants
anything at all. But yes, we need
to stand up for ourselves and those who can't.
God will not pay the bills or extricate
the prisoners who should not be in prison
(for one example). We are responsible
for maintenance of our planet and ourselves.
Who else will care for the poor or the dying
whose throats are dry as drought, whose eyes are sunk
so deep in their sockets they cannot see
the nurse approaching with a wetted sponge?

The *Intellectus*

> "...what can't be changed must be accepted with *a sacrificium intellectus*, although the *sacrificium* is not quite complete, and the *intellectus* silently goes its own way."—*Dietrich Bonhoeffer*

The *intellectus* seeks a way out
whether body can follow or not.
It craves escape. It wants to think
about something besides being in prison.

It thinks of mountains and meadows, of
sweet spring water and cooling off
after the afternoon heat dies down
and a lengthy day turns into evening.

The *intellectus* searches a star-scarred night
remembered and dreamed long ago,
looking for a corner from which
to study light and blackest darkness.

It finds a nook behind a planet,
curls up as if to sleep then thinks
some more as that is all it can do.
Nevertheless, it's free and safe

and can think whatever it wishes to.

Happiness

"What is happiness and unhappiness? It depends so little on the circumstances; it depends really only on that which happens inside a person."—*Dietrich Bonhoeffer*

He wrote these words to his Maria while
imprisoned. One biographer suggests
Dietrich's true love was his colleague Bethge.
He did love Bethge, but he also loved
the lovely Maria. Perhaps his love for her
was idealized—how otherwise,
given the distance between them and their ages—
but Maria was too intelligent not
to understand what was expected of her
and he too intelligent not to see
that she was a person in her own right.
So what is love? Less a rose, I think,
than the headstrong weed that grows despite
a hampering lack of water or little light.

Toothpaste and a Few Coffee Beans—*From his last letter to his parents*

He asked his aging parents to send
toothpaste and a few coffee beans.
Also, Plutarch's *Lives of Great Men.*

What do we call a great man now?
Dietrich Bonhoeffer? Possibly so,
though plans to disrupt The Fuhrer Show

went awry. Still, he tried
where most did not, where most followed
the madman—as if Hitler were a guide

to anything but blind destruction,
including his own suicide.
Toothpaste and coffee make the morning sun

brighter even when it rains.
He ran his tongue over his teeth
and drank his coffee, content with small gains.

Human Relationships

> "In the long run, human relationships are the most important thing in life. . .[W]hat is the finest book, or picture, or estate, to me, compared to my wife, my parents, or my friend?"—*Dietrich Bonhoeffer*

I know I should agree. It's not as if
I don't remember what it's like to live
alone, to be a rotten failure at
everything human. But I love the art
of putting words in places where they rhyme
or forge a sentence that may surprise or sing
or function as a stepping stone to structure.
I love the miniature dilemmas of
punctuation and the infinite
dimensions of syntax while subordinate
clauses, or simple phrases, twist and turn
over endlessly, endlessly, music
that remakes itself new with each new creation.

Dietrich walked with Christ in Gethsemane.
I am merely one of those women who
are said to scribble. He took up the cross
Christ carried to Golgotha and consoled
Christ's mother at the skull-strewn base of her son's
crucifixion. Who am I? Nobody,
as Emily Dickinson herself said,
and probably I do not deserve to be read,
and yet I too have been blessed by the German pastor
who fully believed what I cannot believe.
His name is rightly written in the book of life.

That Old-Time Religion

That old-time religion, he said, had to go—
was already, said the pastor, gone.
Only the personal encounter with God
defined an individual as Christian.

"Personal encounter" meant reliving
the torments Jesus suffered. Which were those
the Jews were made to suffer. Which had bound
modern man to history and the world.

The Christian, he said, was "simply a human being,"
as was Jesus, aware of what one's life
must mean. Aware also of certain death
and—this is where I bow out—resurrection.

To follow Jesus was to live for others—
the aging neighbor, the ailing friend, all those
who'd benefit from a hand on a shoulder.
Such was his vision of Christianity

now that it had been reduced by the Nazis.
Then papers were found, confirming the plot against Hitler—
the particular plot that included the German pastor.
Worried his family might have to endure

retribution, he abandoned his plan to escape.
The brutal hanging Hitler ordered ensured
that Dietrich Bonhoeffer would suffer in the extreme.
Transferred to an SS prison, he was separated

from his Bible and subjected to
interrogation and torture conducted by
eager Gestapo. Then two months in Buchenwald
and finally Flossenbürg. Without defense

or testimony, at night, Bonhoeffer was condemned
to death, he and five others commanded at dawn
to strip and march naked to the gallows, arms tied
in back. The next day a fellow prisoner said

he saw a hook, as in a slaughterhouse.
The hanged, he noted, could just barely graze
the ground with their feet, prolonging the men's agony.

This makes me want to weep but I remain
dry-eyed. Weeping never brings anyone back.
There are no miracles in our modern age.

And yet—

And yet perhaps it is a miracle
that a woman without faith can recognize
the miracle of the German pastor's heart.

Thinking Ahead

What would the pastor think of ISIL
these later years? That evil owned
the upper hand? That God had fled
to parts unknown? Probably not.

He'd still find life good and useful
because that was who he was,
a man of the rood. A man of belief.
A man brainwashed by the Bible.

Religion remains a danger to all.
What *is* religion, if not dream
and ignorance, a cheese sandwich
that settles the nervous stomach, not

to mention the nervous brain that thinks
a god can oversee and save
our fretful souls. There is no such.
We are wholly on our own, speeding

through outer space. The human race
is barely holding on.
But what a ride,
what an illuminating ride.

IV.

SISTERS

Sisters

A sister is a part of one's own heart,
ventricle or murmur or the beat
that measures music and our unmetrical lives.

She is as permanent as the telling numbers
imprinted on the underside of wrists
belonging to survivors of the camps.

She's bone of your body, flesh of flesh, someone
who might be you except that she arrived
before or after you, the mirror of

yourself and yet a mirror in which you find
no resemblance to yourself, thoroughly
blinded as you are by closeness and confusion.

She is perceptive and may know much more
about you than you have ever thought but then
what don't you know about your only sister?

A sister's as contingent as oneself
and when she leaves her sister feels the cold
as if it were a season of despair,

as if her sister, a flautist and the gentler
of the pair, took with her what of warmth was left,
what of light, harmony, and prayer.

Lake Rosseau, Canada

When we reached the rented summer house we found chipmunks
camping in the large cheapshit kitchen

Quicksand could swallow you, legs and arms and all,
especially if you were a child, *girl*-child at that

Vampiric leeches latched onto our arms and legs.
Our mother plucked them off, those bloody suckers.

The green rowboat sidled into reeds
or cattails, ferrying sisters on splintery plank seats

On land we sisters took turns climbing into
the washtub to roll sideways down the piney slope

The resinous pines quickened the air and pine
needles fell, a homespun blanket over the hills.

Nights, the cry of the loon crossed over water.
We could tell the man in the moon had a secret.

Families Are War Zones

I wish I'd been a better sister but
Ann stole my father's heart and I was left
empty-handed, caught in raging crossfire
between my mother and my older brother.

My sister did not plan to do it.
My sister was without animus.
I was the one with animosity.
I was the one no one paid attention to,

except sometimes my brother, who, however,
resented having to babysit his sister.
Families are war zones, or was mine
the only one? We could have mapped the Parallel

between ourselves and necessary safety.
My sister never cried in her cradle.
She gurgled happily, her baby hair
a kind of sunlight in the northern city

to which my father's professional ambition
brought us. Ithaca was gray and cold.
We'd come from Baton Rouge. We weren't prepared
for torturous days of darkness. Snow descending

from the air was new to all of us except
our father, who, even so, grew up in
South Carolina. (He studied violin
and theory in Chicago and New York.)

I remember snowflakes spinning around
the street lamp. Ann and I would watch the wind
wrap the street lamp in bright white, from floors
above. The ground floor was a grocery store.

We still shopped with ration stamps. Our mother
still scrubbed clothes on a washboard in the bathtub.
Our mother, second fiddle in the string quartet
and beautiful and intelligent, scarily

so, with energy to burn. My father still
doted on Ann and she became the musician
among the children, though we all loved music.
Why couldn't music bring us all together?

Though I guess it did. Just not enough
to save us from our separate beginnings
and botched attempts to rectify our *days*
and works. Something had gone awry, astray,

and could not be found or fixed. I blame myself,
though that's of little use. And all that music,
all that suasive music we all loved so much—
t might have made our dissonant family

harmonious as Bach.

Not an Accident

The lead car in the stopped lane had stopped,
acknowledging the red light. The light
was still red when the car revved up and tore
across the intersection, where my sister,
student at the Cleveland Institute of Music,
was walking with the greenest of green lights.
It was 1964 and she was twenty.
The car aimed itself straight at her, a car
packed with laughing passengers, as if
this was a party game. My sister said
that she remembered nothing but the blinding
headlights bearing down on her. She tried
to hold onto her flute case but it flew off
like a bird of night rising toward the moon
and diving back to earth. In Virginia,
the phone rang for our parents. Later they said
that night taught them why marriage was for two:
both taking turns falling apart and leaning
on the one who was for the nonce not falling.
Ann's forehead was gone. Her two front teeth gone.
The doctors could not say if she would live.
She did live but they had to find an expert
dentist who could reconstruct her teeth
such that her embouchure, so beautiful,
would be the same as it had been before.
She lost a year to recuperating in
the house in Virginia, watching television
until she thought the images on the screen
were people she knew in the flesh. She was alone all day.
Our parents worked day and night. I was in England,
our older brother Mike in New York City.

That much aloneness was a kind of jail,
as if she and not the guilty driver were
in solitary confinement. For a while
she moved between a made-up world and the one
in which our parents and the house were real,
and when she realized what she was doing
she said she wanted to return to Cleveland
to prove that she could cross that killing road.
Returning was hard. The first time she walked across
that street, terror made her freeze and sweat.
But she was brave. She kept on crossing streets,
flute case in hand. Nothing was going to stop
my sweet and strong-willed sister from making music.
Water from a spring was not more pure
or fresher than the sound of her silver flute.

Abortion

She'd no desire for children. Hated the way
we were brought up, or rather, were not brought up.
Left to roam alone like skittish kittens
without a home, our dreams were filled with tears.
By day, we fought our way at recess through
East Hill Elementary. A kid
at bat on the playground, aiming for the ball
coming straight at him, missed, the bat bashing
        my little sister in the forehead. Meanwhile
I was sent over and over to the principal's office
and Ann thought I reflected poorly upon her.
I probably did. "It was not a normal childhood,"
she would say later, when she was living in London
and I visited. She had dual citizenship
by then. When she married, she sewed the dress,
the wedding dress, baked the wedding cake,
laid the table, and paid for everything.
The groom turned out to be a smalltime criminal.
She kicked him out. Purchased a house for one
(our parents helped) on the far East Side, near
the docks, where she became a fighter for
the rights of working men. There were boyfriends,
one a fat, lazy slob she catered to.
He had a job with British Telephone
but I thought he was using my sister like
a maid. He knocked her up and despite
my sister's feelings about having children
she thought about a little girl with freckles.
She waited for him to offer to marry her.
When he did not, she made an appointment for
an abortion. She informed him he would drive

her to the doctor's office and drive her home
afterward. She was still hoping he'd ask her
to cancel the appointment.
Afterward,
he drove her to her house but he did not
get out of the car. Did not get out of the car!
The shit. The fat, lazy, slobbering shit!
She'd have kept it, she told me, if he wanted
it, the little girl with a splash of freckles.
I still have an image of a little girl in my mind.
She has those freckles and my sister's face.

A Wedding Song for Ann (Her Second Marriage)

A wedding in London,
and there'll be bells
and something blue
(your new silk dress),
and him and you,

of course, and us,
too—sister and friends
to wish you well.

It may rain,
the sky may be gray
as a prime minister's pants,
traffic may be backed up
on the motorway—

Never mind.
Love in London
is a sort of song—

All those *L's!*

May it last
life long.

London 2013

"I've not known how to tell you," she says.
"So I'll blurt it out. Daddy is dying."
My sister speaks in the softest of voices

and I have to tell her our father died
thirty years ago. I fear
that she'll argue this point, but without

blinking she accepts it. She's living
in several different times at once.
To turn from now to then's as easy

as from then to today or tomorrow.
"She's lost her work," I say to my husband,
"her husband, and now her much-loved house"

(she was going into a home for the dying).
I could not stop crying to save my life,
the tears wetting my husband's comforting,

sweatered chest. English step-relatives
politely and quietly moved one by one outside,
like Haydn's players sequentially departing

the stage. She 'd many memories left. Only
time had dropped away, leaving her
slightly uncertain, slightly confused.

"I was no damn good. I've come to terms
with it." "It" is her flute-playing,
at which she excelled. I think depression

is making her say such a thing, and why wouldn't
she be depressed? We lose everything when
we die, unless we think a birthday cake

is waiting for us in Heaven, and who thinks *that*?

The Carers

Each morning Filipina carers plait
my sister's hair into a single braid
that ladders halfway down her back. In front
her hair's swept back, the temples viewable,
pierceable. I want to shield her from harm,
although there is no harm here, only care.
But she is delicate, her bones a bird's
and small and weightless and much too easy to smash.
The carers cluck and coo and take their turns
adorning her with baubles and barrettes.

Outside, the English garden with its singing trees,
the leafy branches thick with garden warblers.

Hospice

We take my sister, who has late-stage Parkinson's
with worsening dementia, in a cab
to see her husband, who is dying of
a cancer of the tongue unless the cause
is cancer of the mouth or of the throat
(for he has both of these as well), and if
it's not the chemotherapy or surgery.
The doctors had him moved to hospice. He
sits on the edge of the bed, his back to us,
to hide his constant spitting. He spits the blood
that floods into his mouth into a bowl,
receptacle that holds the life draining
away drop by agonizing drop.
His son, a man of middle age, maneuvers
my sister's wheelchair to his father's side.
She twists herself like a rubber band.
Her fingers that played the flute on stages around
the world are gnarled and knotted like ropes, the hands
inseparably entwined like honeysuckle
vines. Her Filipina carers dressed her hair
today, a gold and silver plait as if
a metallurgical alchemy might change
the losses of her life to brilliant gain.
Disease will not allow my sister to
                    be still. Her eyes inspect the ceiling, search
the walls, the floor. She tells her husband that
she loves him and he says the same to her.
We are onlookers here, eavesdroppers,
privy to what always should be private.

Twisting and straining, my sister somehow shakes
off her khaki-colored bootie, the right.
Her husband spots it on the floor. As from
a height, for surely a height it is, he leans
down, holding in the blood in his mouth, to grasp
the bootie, then to slip it on the foot
of his wife and my sister and his son's stepmother,
the Prince and Cinderella at the ball.

The Dream

The night her husband died in hospice
she dreamed he woke her saying good-bye.
Her whispered words were calm as bliss.
There were no tears: I looked her in the eye.

You're sure that it was Paul? I asked
to humor her. *Of course,* she said.
He means to wait for me. I gasped.
I have no faith in a quickening of the dead

but neither did I want to trample on
my sister's hope. Nor did I want
my sister to depart this one
life soon, though she was frail and gaunt.

What I wanted was to keep her here
where I could touch and see and hear
my only sister, last relative.
I wanted her to live. To live!

But she did not. She was so tired,
and Paul awaited her. It wasn't long.
Taken in a hurry to hospital,
she aspirated and was gone.

I hope they are together but
I know they're not. I hope they occupy
a world in which the dead are raised
and reunited with their families

and friends and yet I know that they are not.
I hope beyond belief that I'm mistaken
and still I know I'm not. Not mistaken.
Merely, as happens everywhere, forsaken.

At first we think this world bountiful.
Later we discover it's poor and parched.
Our world is stubborn, difficult, and harsh
but, I wish us all the best of luck.

The Remnant

My sister is dead.
I have become half a person.

My sister has no shadow
or the grave hides it.

The process of decomposition
is silent and secret.

I can walk among the stones
of the cemetery but I cannot

visit my sister who is dead,
who is dissolving,

the liquidity of her body
sinking into earth.

I am what remains,
the torn remnant.

Two Years Later

Last night I dreamed about my sister
and how thoroughly I have missed her.
She hadn't time enough to do
all she wanted to.
She never got the pony she wanted.
Undaunted,
she got a motorcycle and rode it
all over London. She stowed it
in her kitchen when she was home,
my little sister, herself a poem,
with hair like Goldilocks',
her house in the East End docks.
Thrown to the ground,
she got back up and back on, the sound
of screeching wheels reverberant
and menacing. She often sent
letters to the British Parliament
on the dockworkers' behalf.
Had my sister gone bananas? daft?
My little sister, a Union organizer!
Five feet two and a Union organizer!
Those workers learned from her,
as did the students who yearned for her
to turn them into flautist stars.
She taught them well, left no scars
on their psyches, touted their talents.
Teaching demands a pinpoint balance
between encouragement and correction,
between the held note and inflection.
Angels adorned her letters home,
sketches of flute-playing angels, some

joyful, others sad, still
others worried. Our parents could tell
before they opened the envelope
whether she was happy and hopeful
or feeling bad. There were angels
on motorcycles. Angels in tears.
Angels with crowns. Angels with spears,
which meant she was ready to fight
for what she'd decided was right.
Parental anxiety was assuaged
the moment our parents gauged
the envelope and that was good,
as parental anxiety rose high as a flood
and threatened to swamp us all,
including Ann and her husband, Paul,
family life a Katrina of fret and despair,
a despoiling of the very air.
The one good thing? That death makes room
for generations yet to be born.
May they be loving and not self-defeating.
May the little one with chocolate on his face
enjoy what he is eating and the small girl
in Rochester, with a small-girl-size toy broom,
sweep away whatever she wants to sweep away,
and may families everywhere savor their own company.

V

THE FORTUNES OF MEN

The Fortunes of Men

Thanks be to God, two become three,
Caring for their child from cradle through youth,
But only God knows the grown man's fate.
Parental guidance prepares him for manhood—
The child is clothed in colorful costumes,
Is taught to walk and talk and obey,
Adored, encouraged, and ever praised.
Yet—mourned by their mothers—some men die young,
As savage wolves separate out and surround
This lad or that, attack, and dismember
His small body limb by motionless limb.
Mere people cannot prevent or alter
The events prepared by purpose divine.
Some men starve, or storms bury them
At sea, and some by spears are slain
In war. A blinded man worries his way
through life, groping. Another, lame,
Becomes bitter and curses his circumstance.
One falls from a tree in a forest, waving
His arms like wings but they are not wings.
His spirit survives to ascend, perhaps,
Or fly far away. And far away,
Estranged or exiled, enduring the opprobrium
Of those fearful of the unfamiliar,
Someone's lost son slumps beneath the burdens
Of hardship, homesickness, hellish loneliness,
Perceived as the bearer of ruinous luck.
Some men will swing slowly from the gallows
Till dead, whereupon darksome birds
Steal the sightless eyes and shred the bodies—
Which cannot fend off these flying thieves,

Which feel nothing, neither hope nor warmth—
Ghostly pale and pirouetting pointlessly
In demon air, their dread names now
Imprecations, unholy and calamitous.
Some are sentenced to be consumed by fire,
Rabid flames flaring red and wild,
Women weeping, watching sons cremated alive,
Charred remains like ashen coals.
Drink swallows others: diabolic reversal,
It maddens men to mindless volubility
And vehemence, provoking swift swords,
Or, if not, it dazes them night and day
And they drink away their drear, reduced lives,
Slow suicide for sure say those who knew them,
Though some will save themselves in time
To prosper and take pleasure in a separate peace,
Encircled by family and serene as the sun
Till the last light of a long day.
Almighty God administers
Just so his godly justice to all,
Meting out our fortunes meager or great.
Such is our human and honorable estate.
A happy childhood to him here; glory
In triumphant battle to that one there;
Great skill in hunting, shrewdness at dice,
Championship swiftly achieved
At chess, to others. Some crave knowledge,
Becoming scholars, discoursing wisely.
And God shall give the gift of working
In gold to him who hammers the metal
For a king's mail-coat and the king will thank him
With acres of land (accepted at once).
A charming fellow cheers on a crowd

Of rowdy ale-guzzlers ranged on benches.
What revelry, what roisterous joy!
At his king's feet one calls forth music
From the lyre's strings, skipping lightly
Through lovely and lively, lissome moods.
—Songs that fetch a fine fee.
One teaches a hawk to trust his arm,
And the proud creature that plies the skies
Bows to the coaxing, courteous hand
That teaches the hawk to take the scraps
Offered, and bide its time in fetters.
His *master's* hand. Multitudes of men
Move over the earth in manifold ways,
Their diverse dispositions designed by God,
Each as carefully carved and placed
As a chess piece on the chessboard.
Therefore must we admit our God
The Master of men, Deity who determines
The fortunes of men.